LIFE IN NUTSHELL

B. SHRUTI

ISBN 979-888606110-9

Contents

About The Writer   *vii*

About The Publication   *ix*

1. 50 Journey From Birth To Death   1

2. Father And Mother   3

3. Friendship   4

4. Mind Is Mirror   5

5. अजबदुनियाकगिजबडॉटकोम   7

6. पापा(डैडी)   9

7. बुज़ुर्गोकएिहमयित   10

8. सत्यवचन   12

9. जिदगीएकसंघर्षहैं   13

10. बलात्कारीमामला   15

11. बेटियां   17

About The Writer

B.Shruti,a 19-year-old girl from Rourkela,Odisha with big dreams in her eyes persuing her graduation at "GOVERNMENT AUTONOMOUS COLLEGE ROURKELA" in {science stream(MATHS HONS)}.She is an fervent lover of the mighty sword and everytime she loved to spend hours playing with alphabets and painting,but now it has become a passion for her instead of mere hobby.Writing gives her solace and provide her calmness.She is working as a Project Head in "THE QUILL PUBLICATION" and also as a compiler in various publication and also as co-author in various anthologies.She also received scholarship of rs.15000 from "Odisha Government".She considers herself as a mere droplet of water in the entire universe of ocean.Her first and last priority is always her family.She just want to thank "RK PUBLICATION" for giving her this golden opportunity.She has always been enthusiastic in her life.Always down for her friends.Exploring the nature soothes her eyes.Looking forward for Being successful in her future

About The Publication

R.K.Publication is an independent Publishing Platform and Writing Coummity along with many more creative people such as a hub of Open Mic event organizers, Dancers,Singers,Painting/Skecthing Artist and Photographers.We promote them through our featuring page rkpublication that is why this is another name for opportunity.It is a family of Hard work,Dedication and Creativity.

R.K. Publication have their own writing community name R.K.Community.They believe that Community that works together-Stay Together,Grow Together.

Therefore welcoming you to R.K. Family

1. 50 JOURNEY FROM BIRTH TO DEATH

A cry come out
With people's noise and shout
Mother's heart filled with love and pamper
Fat and stout father all work is hampered,
"BECAUSE I AM A BABY"
Mother screeches in her voice
"Son, keep your toys."
My naughtiness couldn't be spared
My father's eyes say "Don't dare".
"BECAUSE I AM A CHILD".
Short morning and long nights,
Mother and father irritated of fight.
Phone, funky hair and bikes
Their only motto is likes.
"BECAUSE I AM AN ADOLESCENT"
I am no more a dude,
I have lost my childhood.
Short nights and long mornings,
Because I want to feed my partners with my earnings.
"BECAUSE I AM AN ADULT".
I am taking my last breath,
This is what is death.

Flashing back all the memories,
I will leave this world,no one knows to Devils or to fairies.
"BECAUSE I AM AN OLDMAN OR WOMAN"
Journey from birth to death is hard,
But we should face it like a pard.
A problem in life is an obstacle,
But if you get a life then it is MIRACLE.

2. FATHER AND MOTHER

'FATHER is the SKY',and 'MOTHER is the EARTH'.

To fulfill every need of us from our birth.

'FATHER is an ARTIST', and 'MOTHER is a PAINTER',they give

shape to our life and future.

'FATHER is a CANDLE',and 'MOTHER is its LIGHT'.

They remove the darkness of our life.

'FATHER is THE SUN' and my 'MOTHER is THE MOON'.

They show us the way to be a good person.

'FATHER is the DAY',and 'MOTHER is 'NIGHT. They make our life

complete and bright.

'FATHER is 'GOD',and 'MOTHER is 'GODDESS'.

They are the source of happiness.

'Our aim is to fulfill our parents 'AMBITION'.

3. FRIENDSHIP

Friendship is like a
Bunch of flowers,
Beauty and fragrance it Showers,
Friendship is like a bird in
The sky,
Having no limit to fly high,
Friendship is like a previous stone,
More expensive than a king's throne.
Friendship is full of feelings
And it is one of the rarest blessings.
#JSSSM forever#

4. MIND IS MIRROR

Hey Guys!!!So from where to start....Yahh!!!each and every people know about Imaginations, Identifications But do uh know What is Illusion?It is nothing but a false belief or we can say that a instance of wrong perception of a sensory experience,Or in hindi what we call as 'Bhram'. I raised this word Because,I want to give simple example of our mind...Does Mind go anywhere?No..Mind doesn't go anywhere it is here thinking about something else which is not real, nor your body neither your mind goes anywhere..You are 'deceive' by the Imagination of your mind by sitting in one place and thinking that your mind goes somewhere but you people are so identified and lost which makes you think this...Mind doesn't travel anywhere and this is very much true...Now you people have to understand or find it of your own that why your mind is going on unmanageable, endless thought from which you are identified or imaging the thing which you are not. The moment that comes into your life you get identified or imagined from something you are not...'Believe me' then your mind becomes a non-stop activity or you people are trying to stop your mind and telling that If you all are going to try this for a long or for a millionaire It's not going to be happen. It's not true. If at that time you take away your wrong Ilusions, Identifications, Imaginations and at that moment your Instant reply will be, "Mind is just,like a mirror not saying anything but reflecting each and everything." So Guys, 'Our Mind is here to give us clarity into our life but right now our mind is a huge and huge ball of confusion. Suppose,Now you are trying to meditate but you all are thinking of Cinema hall, Restaurant etc. Now

someone came to you and said think of God....So you people started thinking of God (Shiva and Parvati) then you will find that you go to cinema with God Shiva. Shiva himself taking you to restaurant...This is what your mind is!!!!Full of Identification. So what to do now it's not about to control your mind it's about to bring awareness..Hence to what you are not. You Should Disengage from your mind at that time Once you Disengage from mind for sometime you will Disengage from all your Illusions, Imaginations, Identifications..Because it's the Mind which manufacturers all the identification...

And also yah sometimes Illusions are good Imaginations are good but only sometimes...Or we can say to Help or Improve anyone!!!!

Here's a simple story that how Illusions are sometimes good.....

There were two old men lying in hospital first men near window on bed and second man straight to the first men bed..The Men near window after his lunch always use to describe nature from his window fir his neighbour..Because the second man he was very ill and passed his day only by lying on his back...The first men always tell that How beautiful the Landscape is!!How beautiful the garden is!!He always explained about beautiful flowers,birds,seas, mountains and many more!!! But the fact is The men who is describing about the nature was blind!!!!!he cannot see even a wall..But he describes everything by his Imaginations, Identifications, Illusions for the second men so by listening him so that he can also try to be fit!! Second men by, listening first men The second men also started Imaging the nature and wanted to view with his own eyes!!!!!

So all this was Illusion for both the men which is not real but good...

In total Never ever lost in imagination or illusion.....But sometimes to help other imagination and illusions are good.....

5. अजबदुनियाकगिजबडॉटकोम

हाथमें *MOBILE*,
सामने *COMPUTER* लैपमेंडालकर *LAPTOP.*
कभीहाथोमें *CIGARETTE* याचाय,
महुमँडालकर *LOLLYPOP...*
करगरदनकोटढी,
करसेडक़पार।
बातोमेंहेंमैशगुल ,
भुलाजीवनअधार।
FRIEND संगघूमाकर,
माँकोबताएकॉलेज।
कहतीमाँमेंपेढरहीहुँ,
बढारहीहुँ *KNOWLEDGE* ।
COMPUTER परटकिटबनता,
हवाई-जहाजयार्टने।
कैसाअजबतकनीकहैयह ,
कैसागजबबब्रने।
कान्हानजेबमहुँखेंलाथा ,
दखिथापुराब्रहमाण।
आजलैपटॉपपरवशिवदखेनका ,
पुराहोताअरमान।
दूरवदिशेमबेंटा-बटीमाँकामनउदास ,
नीरबहदोननीसंकेबहोगीमनकीपुरीआश।

खोलो *INTERNET* जाओ *SKYPE* पेकेरबातेंदेलिखोलकर ,
दखोकैसेवेरेहतेहेंमैनबहलाओहंसबोलकर।
पहलजेबमाँकनिनीमरीथी,
खबरआईथीदसदनिबाद।
तबतकनानीस्वर्गपहुँचकर ,
कथीसबकोवहीसियाद।
अबतोभैयादससेकंडमेंआतीहैं,
न्यूज़गुडऔरबैड ,
खुशीयागमकमेारसेबकोईहोजाता *TOTAL MAD* ।
धीरजरखनाकर्ंटोलकरनासबचीजोंका *SIDE EFFECT* ,
गुडसाइडकोबचाकर ,
रहनाहोगाहमें *PERFECT* .

6. पापा(डैडी)

यहकवतिाउनकेनाम,
जनिसेहेमाराहरदनिहैं......
होतेहैंसेपनहेमार,
परराहदखिातहेंपैापा.
पापाहैतोसारसेपनहेैं,
पापाहैतोबाजारकसेारखेलिौनअपनहैं........
कभीलगीजोठोकरयाचोटतो "ओमाँ" हीमुहँसेनेकिलताहो
लेकनिरास्तापारकरतकेोईटुक्पासआकरब्रेकेलगाएतो "बापरे"
यहीमुहँसेनेकिलताहैं........
मेलेकेभीडम्ें,
कंधेपेरउठातेहेंपैापा,
सीनेपेरबठिाकरखेलखलिातेहेंपैापा..
पापाकतिनेअच्छेहोतेहैं,
परविारकागुरूरऔरहम्मितहोतेहैं....
कनिशबद्ोमंेकेरूुनकाधन्यवाद,
नहींमलिरहहेंैशब्दमुझे,
शब्दोमंेहेंवैाद-वविाद।

• 9 •

7. बुज़ुर्गोंकिएहमयित

'जिसराश्तिकेबिातहोनेजारहीहैं'
उन्हेबसअपनेपनकिआदतहैं'
इसराश्तिकेबारमेंऔरजानतेहैं'
आइएआपकास्वागतहैं',
'हैंयेराश्तिासबसेप्यारा
माँबापसेभीगहरा
सबसेअनोखासबसेन्यारा.
कहतेहैंहररास्तिकेअपनीएहमयितहोतीहैं',
परयेजोरास्तिाहैं'
इनकीबातहिअलगहोतीहैं'.
'जिनकिहोतेहैंदादा-दादी
वोहोतेहैंख़ुशनसीब.
उनकीज्ञान,उनकीसंस्कार
सेहोतीहैंहमारीजीत,
'दादा-दादीहमसेभालंकर'
अपनीफर्जअदाकरतेहैं'
जबहमारीबारीआईतो
हमशेइतनीसीफर्जअदानहोपाई'...
उनकेबिनिाघरअधूरा
उनकेबिनिापरविारअधूरा
कैसेछोड़आतेहैंउन्हेवृद्धआश्रामम
होजातीहैंउनकेबिनिाजीवनअधूरा'...

'क्याजमानाआगयाहै
पहलेउनकेसाथनाहोनेपर
सबकीदलिखटकतीथी
अबउनकेसाथहोनेपरउनकीमौजूदगीपर,
सबकीदलिरोतीहै.
'जबओल्डइजगोल्डकहतेहैंतो
बुजूरगकोगोल्डकतिरहक्योनहींरखते
गोल्डकाध्यानरखाजाएतोलाभहीलाभ...
वैसेबुजूरगकाध्यानरखाजाएतोज्ञानहिज्ञान'...
'बुजूरगोककिरइज्ज़त
हमारीइज्ज़तऔरबढ़जाएगी
इसदेखकर
नईपीढीभीकुछसीखजाएगी'..

8. सत्यवचन

** 'पहला सत्य'
हम जब दिन की शुरूआत करते हैं,
तब लगता है कैसी है ही जीवन है......
लेकिन,
जब शाम को
लौटकर घर आते हैं,
तब लगता है ऐसा ं ती ही जीवन है........
** 'दूसरा सत्य'
भाई द्वारा रावण का साथ न देने पर,
रावण कहता है,
अंदरूनी, एकता बनाए रखो, क्योंकी
किसी भी पेड़ को कटने का किस्सा
न होता, अगर कुल्हाड़ी के पीछे
लकड़ी का हिस्सा न ही होता।
** 'तीसरा और कड़वा सत्य'
"अनाथ आश्रम में बेच्च मिलते हैं गरीबों के" और...
'वृद्धा आश्रम में बेज़ुर्ग मिलते हैं अमीरों के'.

९.जिंदगीएकसंघर्षहै

*जिंदगीएकडोरहै

जहाँबहुतसाराशोरहै

जिंदगीकिआनंदउठानासखिए

वरनाजिंदगीबोरहै

जिंदगीएकसंघर्षहै

हरपलउससेलड़नासखि

दुखदपलकोभी

खुशीसेबितानासखि

है चालाकियोंकाशहर

है पैसोंकाशहर

कसीसेकिसीकउननतदिखीनहींजाती

देखीजातीहैतोसिर्फबरबादीदेखीजातीहै

लोगोंनेदिलतोड़ा

लोगोंनेसाथछोड़ा

लोगोंनेविश्वासतोड़ा

जिंदगीनेमुझंमोड़ा,

जमानाकेसाथजिंदगीबदलरहीहै

वक्तकेसाथइंसानबदलरहहैं,

उम्मीदथीअच्छेलोगोंकेमेलनेकी

उम्मीदथीजिंदगीकोगलेलगानेकी

उम्मीदनहींथीगरिगटिकेतरहलोगमिलेंगे,

उम्मीदतोयेभीनहींथीकपिलभरमंजिंदगीबदलेंगे

हंसाकरेलूलाकेबहुतकुछसखिजातीहैजिंदगी,.
बहुतकुछबाकीरहताहै
*यूहीखत्महोजातीहैजिंदगी।**

10. बलात्कारीमामला

"आजबातकरतेहैंइसमुद्दपेर "
कलकोकहींवक़्तनबदलजाए,
वक़्ततोतजीसनेकिलजाताहैं
"कलकोकहींबलात्कारीबातहनिटालदजिए.....
*अगरदेशककिान्नूनऔरध्यानदती,
तोहरदूसरघरकलिडकीनरिभयानहींहोती..
कलनरिभयाथीआजपुरयिंकारडेडीहैकलकोईऔरहोगी,
देशवासयिोअगरहममजबूतहोजाएतोइंसाफआसानीसेहोगी..
बेटेयिांदरिंदोंकेजालमेंफँसीक्यों
नमानवतारहा, नवशि्वासरहा, सच्चाईनरहाक्यों!
वशि्वासकनेामपरवशि्वासघातीलोग
वशि्वासघातीपरवशि्वासक्यों!
जन्मदतेहैंलाडोबटियिाँको
फरिउन्हींकेसाथदरदिंगीक्यों..
चुप्पीवक़्तकेसाथआदतबनजाएगी,
राततडाकीचीखोंसेभरजाएगी,
क्यामरेीलाडोघरकेबेाहरनहींजाएगी..
बार-बारलूटरहींहैं
जार-जारलूटरहींहैं
क्योंचीखताबचपनसहमगईथीलाडो..
हैवानयितऔरसरकारीचोंचलनेसमझतीलाडो,
डरकसेहमकदेर-दरभटकतीलाडो,

इंसाफ़चाहिएइंसाफ़चाहिएकहकरदेशसेलड़तीलाडो!!!
"सच्चाईकउिम्मीदरखहेकिसिसे
जबदेशकाका़नूनखुदबकिाहुआहै..
अगरवोउनकीखुदकबिटिीहोती
तबफांसीभीनहीरुकाहुआहै"!!
येलाडोहमारीनहीतुम्हारीनहीपूरीदेशकहिैं...
इसलिएइन्हेंसंभालकररखनाचाहिए।भीकमांगतेहुएभारतमासँेकहतीलाडो....
कहिमेंआजादीचाहिए*।

11. बेटियां

*बोयेजाएहैंबेटे,
परउगाएजातीहैंबेटियां
-खड़पानीबेटेको,
परलहरतीहैंबेटियां
स्कूलजातेहैंबेटे,
-परपढ़जातीहैंबेटियां
मेहनातकरतहेबेटे,
-परअव्वलआतीहैंबेटियां
नामकरनेंकरेंबेटेपर,
-नामकमातीहैंबेटियां
जबदर्ददतेहैंबेटे,
-तबमरहमलगातीहैंबेटियां
छोडजातेहैंजबबबेटे,
तोसाथनिभातीहैंबेटियां
आशारहतीहैबेटेसे,
परपूरणकरतहिबेटियां
हजारोफरमायिशेंभराहैबेटे,
परसमयकीनजाकतकोसमझतीहैंबेटियां
बेटेकोचांदजैसामतबनाओ
कीहरकोईघोर-घूरकदेखे,,
बेटीकीसूरजजैसाबनाओ
तकीघुरनेसेपहलसबकीनजरझुकजाये॥